LIGHTNING BOLT BOOKS™

Meet a Baby Cow

Buffy Silverman

Lerner Publications ◆ Minneapolis

To Emma,
Moo from Mom

Lerner Publications Company
A division of Lerner Publishing Group, Inc.
241 First Avenue North
Minneapolis, MN 55401 USA

For reading levels and more information, look up this title at www.lernerbooks.com.

Library of Congress Cataloging-in-Publication Data

Names: Silverman, Buffy, author.
Title: Meet a baby cow / Buffy Silverman.
Description: Minneapolis : Lerner Publications, [2016] | Series: Lightning bolt books. Baby farm
    animals | Audience: Ages 5–8. | Audience: K to grade 3. | Includes bibliographical references
    and index.
Identifiers: LCCN 2015033972| ISBN 9781512407983 (lb : alk. paper) | ISBN 9781512410266 (eb pdf)
Subjects: LCSH: Calves—Juvenile literature. | Cows—Juvenile literature.
Classification: LCC SF205 .S56 2016 | DDC 636.2/07—dc23

LC record available at http://lccn.loc.gov/2015033972

Manufactured in the United States of America
1 – BP – 7/15/16

Table of Contents

Welcome to the World

Soon a new baby will join the farm. This mother cow is about to give birth! A baby cow grows inside its mom for about nine months.

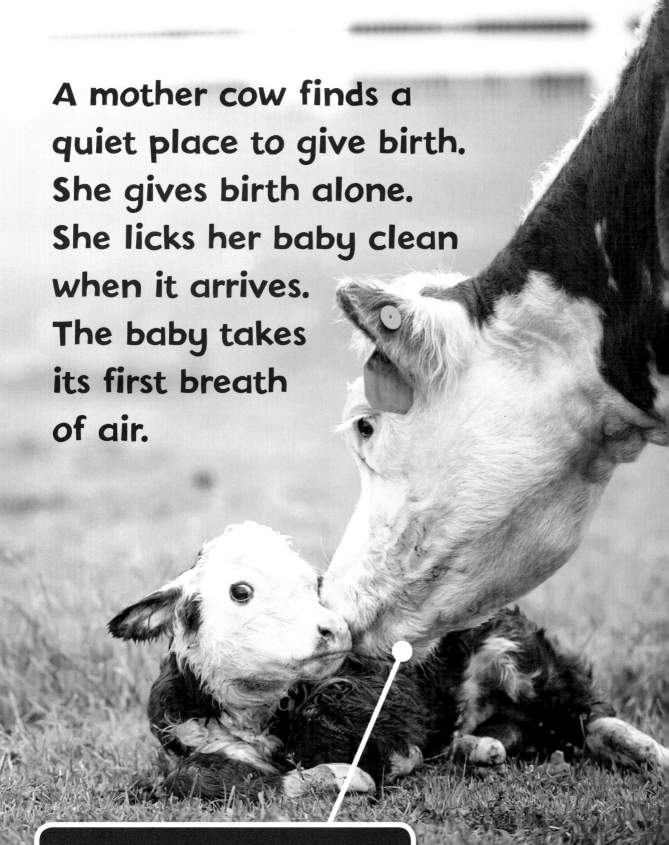

A mother cow finds a quiet place to give birth. She gives birth alone. She licks her baby clean when it arrives. The baby takes its first breath of air.

A mother cow licks her baby. A baby cow is called a calf.

Mother and baby get to know each other. They learn the smell, sight, and sound of each other. The mother and baby bond.

This cow sniffs her calf.

A mother cow nudges her calf. The calf stands for the first time.

Calves stand soon after they are born.

A calf has its first meal when it is about two hours old. It sucks milk from its mother's teats.

A mother cow's milk is very good for her baby. The milk has nutrients that keep the calf healthy.

Nutrients are things like vitamins and minerals. Nutrients help calves grow.

A newborn calf is skinny. It weighs about as much as a fourth grader.

An adult cow is huge. It can weigh more than sixteen fourth graders!

Staying Close to Mom

A calf needs lots of milk to grow. A calf nurses four or five times a day!

This calf is nursing, or drinking milk from its mother.

A calf follows its mother.
The cow protects her calf.
She chases away animals
that might hurt her calf.

Mother cows keep a close lookout for danger.

Sometimes a mother cow hides her calf in tall grass. The calf rests while the cow grazes. Young calves rest for many hours each day.

Calves are harder to spot with tall grass around them.

The mother returns to the place where she left her calf. She calls to her calf. *Menh,* replies the hungry calf.

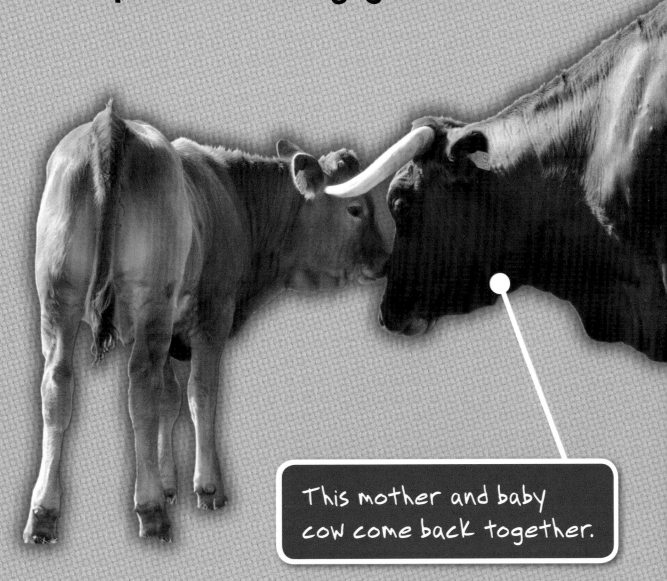

This mother and baby cow come back together.

Cows live in a group called a herd. The cows care for all the calves in the herd. Group living helps keep calves safe.

Sometimes a calf tries to nurse from a cow that is not its mom. The mother cow lets only her calf nurse from her. She pushes other calves away.

A mother cow won't allow calves that aren't hers to nurse from her. But she cares for all the calves in her herd.

Chewing, Chewing, Chewing

A calf stays near its mom for its first six months. It nurses when it is hungry.

Calves stay near their moms as they grow.

This calf is beginning to graze.

At two months old, a calf learns to graze. It puts its muzzle close to the ground. It twists grass around its tongue. It cuts plants with its lower teeth.

Cows have four parts in their stomachs. The parts are called chambers. Grass is broken down partway in the first two chambers.

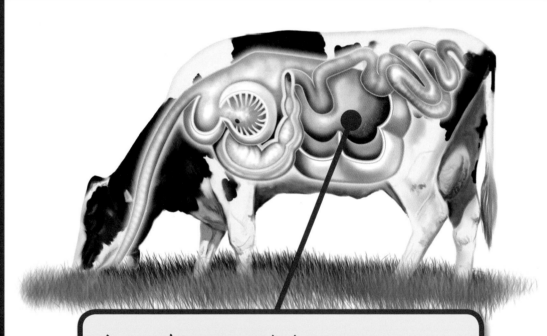

A cow's stomach has more parts than a person's stomach.

Then the calf throws the food up into its mouth. The food is now called cud. The calf chews and swallows its cud. It moves into the last two stomach chambers. There it is broken down further.

This cow is chewing its cud.

As a calf gets older, it spends more time with other calves. Calves play together. They run and jump. They lick and smell one another. They learn to care for themselves.

A group of calves stands together.

705

709

Joining the Herd

Calves learn their place in a herd. Older animals get better grazing spots than young ones.

Some cows in a herd get better grazing spots than others.

Six-month-old calves graze for six hours or more each day. They bite tender young plants. They graze in sunshine and in rain.

Calves stick their muzzles into water. They suck it up. They drink many gallons of water each day.

A female calf stops nursing when it is around eight months old. A male stops nursing by eleven months old. They spend their days grazing. Soon they will be old enough to mate.

These young cows eat together.

A two-year-old cow moos quietly. She stands alone. She is ready to give birth to her first calf!

Why People Raise Cows

About 1.4 billion cattle live on farms around the world. People drink milk from cows that are raised on dairy farms. Most cheese and yogurt are made from cows' milk. Cattle are raised on farms and ranches for beef. Leather for belts, shoes, clothing, wallets, furniture, and footballs comes from cowhide. People make many other products from cow parts. These include oil, soap, medicine, lipstick, and even fireworks. Cow horns, hooves, and bones are made into buttons, glue, combs, toothbrushes, and violin strings.

Fun Facts

- Female cattle that have not given birth are called heifers. After giving birth, a female is called a cow. An adult male is usually called a bull. But people often use the word *cow* to refer to both male and female cattle.

- A cow must give birth before she can make milk. Cows on dairy farms have a calf every twelve to fourteen months. A five-year-old cow can make 12 gallons (45 liters) of milk a day.

- Calves on dairy farms don't usually nurse from their mothers. They are fed from bottles instead.

Glossary

bond: to form a close relationship

calf: a young cow or bull

chamber: an enclosed space

cud: food brought up into the mouth from part of a cow's stomach to be chewed again

graze: to feed on grass and other plants

herd: a group of animals of the same kind that live together

muzzle: the nose and mouth of an animal

nurse: to drink milk from a mother's body

nutrient: a vitamin, mineral, or other substance that is good for health

teat: a part of a cow's body through which milk is sucked

Further Reading

All about Cows for Kids
http://www.kiddyhouse.com/Farm/Cows
/cows.html

Barnyard Palace: Dairy Cows
http://www.ncagr.gov/cyber/kidswrld/general
/barnyard/dairybn.htm

I Didn't Know That: Milking a Cow
http://video.nationalgeographic.com/video/i-didnt
-know-that/idkt-milking-cow

Sexton, Colleen A. *The Life Cycle of a Cow.*
Minneapolis: Bellwether Media, 2011.

Taus-Bolstad, Stacy. *From Grass to Milk.*
Minneapolis: Lerner Publications, 2013.

Index

Photo Acknowledgments

The images in this book are used with the permission of: © Smileus/Thinkstock, p. 2;
© iStockphoto.com/hidesy, p. 4; © iStockphoto.com/emholk, p. 5; © ermess/
Shutterstock.com, p. 6; © iStockphoto.com/vandervelden, p. 7; © Jesus Keller/
Shutterstock.com, p. 8; © M. Rohana/Shutterstock.com, p. 9; © Fuse/Thinkstock, p. 10;
© naumoid/Thinkstock, p. 11; © Musat/Thinkstock, p. 12; © iStockphoto.com/
melissatenpas, p. 13; © bruce m long/Bigstock.com, p. 14; © Age fotostock/SuperStock,
p. 15; © iStockphoto.com/doug4537, p. 16; © Jenifer Harrington/The Image Bank/Getty
Images, p. 17; © iStockphoto.com/mountainberryphoto, p. 18; © Top Photo Group/
Thinkstock, p. 19; © iStockphoto.com/nicolasprimola, p. 20; © iStockphoto.com/
rclassenlayouts, p. 21; © lillisphotography/Getty Images, p. 22; © iStockphoto.com/
venemama, p. 23; © Melissa Carrol/E+/Getty Images, p. 24; © COMPAGNON Bruno/
SAGAPHOTO.COM/Alamy, p. 25; © meteo021/Thinkstock, p. 26; © Stock Connection/
SuperStock, p. 27; © iStockphoto.com/driftlessstudio, p. 29; © iStockphoto.com/tamer,
p. 30.

Front cover: © Nate Allred/Shutterstock.com.

Main body text set in Johann Light 30/36.